# Prompt Me
## Creative Writing Journal & Workbook

By
Robin Woods

EPIC

# Epic Books Publishing

A boutique publishing company
Visit us at: www.epicbookspublishing.com

Lead editor: Beth Braithwaite
Other editing: Tamar Hela
Beta Reader: Tessa Larrabee

Copyright © 2016 Robin Woods, First Edition
Updated 2019

Cover Design created on Canva by Robin Woods

All Photos taken by Robin Woods
Photo Notes: 3. San Jose, CA with Mount Umunhum in the background 5. Downtown Seattle, Washington 6. An elephant in Kruger National Park in South Africa 8. A subway escalator under Seattle, WA 11. Florence, OR 12. Siuslaw River Bridge in Florence, OR

Fonts: Century, Gothic Ultra

Summary: A wide variety of writing prompts for maximum inspiration.

[Creative Writing, Diary, Non-Fiction, Reference, Writing Workbook, Fiction Writing, Writing Journal]

ISBN-10: 1-941077-09-9
ISBN-13:978-1-941077-09-2

# Table of Contents

Introduction ................................................................ 7

How to Use This Book .................................................. 7

Picture Prompts ........................................................... 9

Story Starters: First Person ........................................ 57

Story Starters: Third Person ....................................... 73

Use These Phrases ...................................................... 85

Choose a Path .............................................................. 91

Chart It ........................................................................ 99

Dialogue Prompts ...................................................... 115

Fill in the Blank: 49 Possibilities ............................. 125

Traditional Prompts ................................................... 131

    Self-Discovery ...................................................... 133

    If You Were ........................................................... 135

    Mixed Bag ............................................................. 136

    Make a List Of... ................................................... 137

Haiku .......................................................................... 145

Journal ........................................................................ 149

Reference .................................................................... 161

    Character Traits ................................................... 163

    Character Appearance Charts .............................. 164

    Avoid Language that Offends .............................. 165

    Strong Words to Know and Use ........................... 166

    Tastes and Aromas .............................................. 167

    Words for Sounds ................................................ 168

    Synonyms .............................................................. 169

Books by Robin Woods ............................................... 175

About the Author ........................................................ 176

# Introduction

When taking pictures for this workbook, I came across this stacked wood in a wild array of colors. Part of it reminded me of a pile of books and the other part of an artist's palette—wild hues in haphazard designs that were used to create something else very beautiful. That is much like writing.

Writing is sometimes messy, and sometimes we need a little help even getting to the mess. When you begin to form your ideas, don't worry about grammar and punctuation. Simply getting the words down and experimenting is the most important part in the beginning. In order to become a better writer, you need to do three things:

1. Write often.

2. Read often.

3. Don't be afraid to make mistakes.

Embrace the mess and find your voice. Because as Maya Angelou once said:

"There is no greater agony than bearing an untold story inside you."

Think of these pages as your artist's studio. Experiment with color and style. You never know; you may start something that grows into a masterpiece.

# How to Use This Book

There are a variety of different styles of prompts in this workbook to help you decide what works best for you. If one style or prompt doesn't work, move on. If it doesn't work for you today, it might tomorrow.

If the pronouns don't work for you, change the she to a he, or vice versa. Prompts are meant to be inspiration not shackles.

Carry it around with you. Mess it up. Use different kinds of ink. Stick Post-Its all over it.

Now, go forth and write!

# Picture Prompts

It has often been said that a picture is worth a thousand words—but that doesn't really help writers. However, a picture can inspire thousands of words.

Use the photos to create a unique story.

## Writing Challenge:

Use at least three of the five senses in each of your stories.

☐ Sight   ☐ Taste   ☐ Touch   ☐ Smell   ☐ Sound

There are charts in the reference section in the back.

## 1. Title: _____

## 2. Title: _____

## 3. Title: _____

4. Title: _____

# 5. Title: _____

## 6. Title: _____

## 7. Title: _____

## 8. Title: _____

## 9. Title: _____

## 10. Title: _____

## 11. Title: _____

## 12. Title: _____

## 13. Title: _____

## 14. Title: _____

## 15. Title: _____

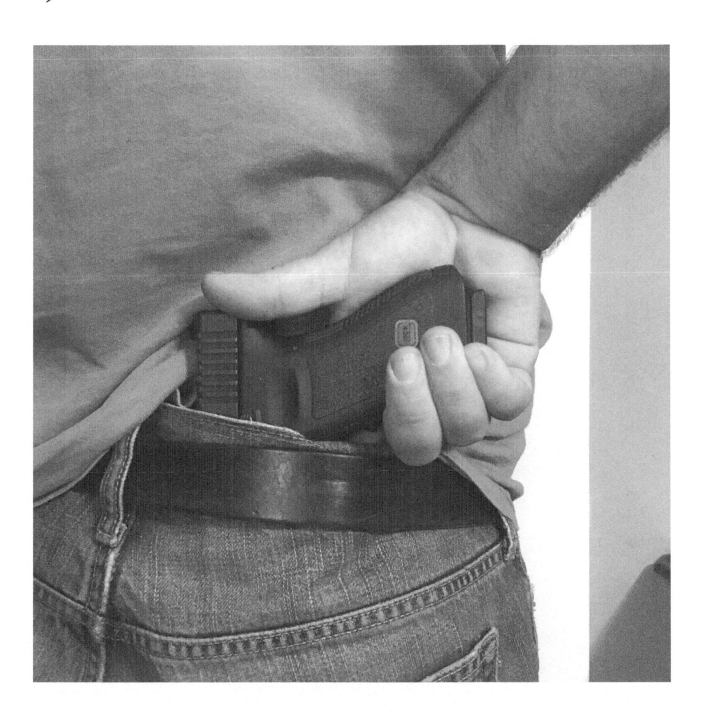

# Story Starters: First Person

Emotional Standpoint: Subjective
View: Limited
Pronoun Usage: I/we/us/me/my/mine/our/ours

## Writing Challenge:

Vary your sentence beginnings by limiting the number of sentences you start with "I" and "The."

# First Person

16. The sword felt foreign in my hand, but as the sound grew closer...

17. The great hall was teaming with suitors from the far reaches of...

18. A murder of crows hung low in the tree as we passed into...

19. Even with my eyes shut, the light made me flinch away...

20. Rumors were that this was the real deal, just like the Oracles in Greek myths. I entered...

21. Cringing, I sniffed at the...

22. Whoever it was, they were lying alarmingly still. I didn't know whether to...

23. When his lips met mine, a nervous giggle escaped...

24. I rubbed the fluid between my fingertips, but I couldn't place...

25. Her voice trembled. "If I had known all of you were going to arrive, I would have prepared. Forgive me."

26. When I popped the trunk, I jumped back...

27. I stomped on the brakes, but the pedal went clear to the floor.

28. The sound of the engine lulled me until the train conductor blasted the horn...

29. I couldn't handle the rattling any longer. I pulled to the side of the road and...

30. The "fasten seat belt" lights started dinging at the same moment the Captain's voice boomed over the intercom. I...

31. We lurched forward, and the engine shuddered to a stop as...

32. I jumped as if I had been doing something wrong, but...

33. Palming the memory stick, I weaved my way through the chattering crowd...

34. The police didn't understand what was coming for them; I had to get out...

35. My face was burning with embarrassment. I tried to keep my voice steady when...

36. To my relief, the snow was covering my footsteps. Though, if their tracker was as good as I'd thought, it wouldn't take long...

37. We were out of wood. I froze, wondering how we would...

38. I carefully folded the chocolate into the mixture with the precision of a...

39. The sound in my ears warbled, and the hair on my neck pricked as...

40. "No! Absolutely not! I am not in love with him/her." Then I realized my voice was way too loud and way too defensive...

41. I stared at the oncoming clouds—this was not good. Turning on my heel, I sprinted to...

42. No matter how hard I tried, my feet couldn't find purchase. Panic set in and my palms began to sweat...

43. He scoffed at me. "Was that supposed to hurt?"
    I set my jaw and answered through my teeth. "That...

44. I leaned back, cradling my head in my hands. This was definitely worth all the...

45. "Ha, those don't exist." But my voice wasn't confident. I couldn't deny all the things I'd just seen.

46. Happiness had always seemed elusive to me, but today, everything was different...

47. When I returned to the table, he was gone. I searched the restaurant—nothing. I didn't know if I should be offended or worried...

48. Zombies? Really? I had thought those were all played out. Gripping the club...

49. The television had been droning in the corner all day, but I couldn't will myself to move...

50. He was hitting on me in the frozen food aisle? How cliché could he be? I grabbed a Healthy Choice meal and...

51. When the sun eased over the mountain tops in an amazing burst of color, the relief was palpable. We had survived. Hearing something behind me, I spun...

52. She hitched her thumb over her shoulder in my direction. "He's delusional. He thinks he's on a mission from God."

53. The knock at the door jarred me from sleep. I tripped my way to the door, noticing that my living room was filled with red and blue light...

54. I scratched behind my ear. "I don't know. It was a really weird dream. I was hanging out with Britney Spears at the Super Bowl, and someone stole my wallet...

55. The cold started getting to me. I slid the hundredth board under the chop saw and started to make the cut, but this time...

56. Sucking it up, I took the plunge. "Hey, you think you wanna get coffee sometime? No pressure or anything. I just thought...

57. The sun dipped below the horizon, and the landscape was bathed in amber. It reminded me of when I was younger and...

58. *Well, that was a terrible way to die.* I dusted myself off and prepared to try again.

59. The imposter was sleeping on the cot next to me; something in me made me wonder if he was aware that his cover was blown. I slid my hand...

60. *I hate holidays.* The present was crushed under my booted foot as...

61. When the screaming started, the smart thing to have done would have been to run away from the noise. I sighed and sprinted, cursing myself as I did. *I am* so *not smart.*

62. "You know that's poisonous, right?" I took a lofty step back.

63. "How long 'til they come for us?"

    I shrugged, measuring my response. "An hour—maybe..."

64. I was innocent, but what did they care?

65. Stopping short, I stared at the shiny new lock, completely dumbfounded. I yanked at it, knowing it was useless. Glancing from side to side, I pulled out...

Prompt # _____ Your Title: _____

Prompt # _____ Your Title: _____

Prompt # _____ Your Title: _____

Prompt # _____ Your Title: _____

_____

_____

_____

_____

_____

_____

_____

_____

_____

_____

_____

_____

_____

_____

_____

_____

_____

_____

_____

_____

_____

_____

_____

_____

Prompt # _____ Your Title: _____

Prompt # _____ Your Title: _____

Prompt # _____ Your Title: _____

Prompt # _____ Your Title: _____

_____

_____

_____

_____

_____

_____

_____

_____

_____

_____

_____

_____

_____

_____

_____

_____

_____

_____

_____

_____

_____

_____

_____

_____

Prompt # _____ Your Title: _____

Prompt # _____ Your Title: _____

Prompt # _____ Your Title: _____

# Story Starters:
# Third Person

**Third Person Limited**
Emotional Standpoint: Objective
View: Limited
Pronoun Usage: he/she/it/him/his/her/they/their

**Third Person Omniscient**
Emotional Standpoint: Objective
View: Unlimited
Pronoun Usage: he/she/it/him/his/her/they/their

**Deep Third Person**
Emotional Standpoint: Subjective
View: Limited
Pronoun Usage: he/she/it/him/his/her/they/their

# Third Person

66. She woke, springing to her feet, but her wrist was...

67. He staggered, listing to the side like a ship in troubled water. Then...

68. Water rushed inside, so cold she gasped, trying to keep...

69. Flies swirled in a horrible buzz. The only thing worse was the smell of the...

70. Mud slurped at his boots...

71. The air would only last a few more minutes...

72. Lightning lit the room, and in that flash, he realized he wasn't alone...

73. The mansion stood on the lonely shore and beckoned to her, despite the simultaneous feeling that she should run. She found herself...

74. He smacked his lips as if there was a bad taste in this mouth. "It's on a CD-ROM? How 2005 of you."

75. Leisurely, his lips curled into a grin. "You think I'm a hostage?"

76. She dropped onto her haunches. "Are you okay, sweetie?"

77. Rainwater was soaking through his trench coat as he labored down the darkened street. Each breath was becoming more difficult...

78. Looking up, she realized the woman standing directly in front of her could've been her twin. Then it sunk in—the stranger was dressed exactly like her. When she turned to...

79. Dr. Rankin closed his clipboard with a snap. "I'm sorry. We simply don't know...

80. He tipped his hat back on his head. "You said that you believe all is fair in love and war. Well, according to that, this is fair."

81. It reminded her of a nebula. When a hand clamped her shoulder, she realized that she'd been overly focused. Now...

82. Fantasy and reality became blurred. He rubbed at his chest; the burning was getting worse...

83. He had to find out who had murdered him before he died. (Note: Pronouns are referring to the same person)

84. She glanced out the window. "What are soldiers doing at the school?" she whispered to her lab partner.

85. "You need to work out more."
Her eyes bugged. "I'm six months pregnant."

86. *Surviving the apocalypse was easy compared to this*, he thought. He pressed the wad of bandages to his side and...

87. A burst of heat from the fire made her eyes water. She wiped them with...

88. They weren't all going to make it...

89. Squeals of joy and terror surged from the carnival ride as the leather...

90. *They were sentient.* He blinked at the epiphany—everything they'd been told was wrong.

91. The prey came into range...

92. It was the third time that she'd seen him today.

93. Her feet were blistered, and she wasn't sure how much longer...

94. "Are you sure it was terrorism?" the agent asked.

95. When he stomped the brakes, the tires locked up. The stupid kid in front of him was talking on his cell phone...

96. Wasting good flowers seemed a crime, but there was no way...

97. She cursed, then growled, "I hate squirrels."

98. He dusted off his pants. *Does the hero always win?* He was about to find out.

99. Sweeping her arm around the landscape, she said, "This used to be the North Sea."

100. The shattered mirror fragments stared back with a thousand eyes...

101. She read the bottle: "Uncork me and make a wish."

102. "Whatever this is, it isn't from Earth. This isn't even on the periodic table."

103. He had to get out; if he wasn't at the location for the next time shift, he would be stuck here forever.

104. This was the fifth night in a row she had been perched in this booth eating the same exact meal.

105. "An arranged marriage? Are you kidding me? I thought those went out a century ago."

106. His neighbors had thought he was crazy for building a bomb shelter…

107. When they opened the door, there was a small, shivering mass huddled in the corner…

108. Zombies were the least of their worries…

109. "So, what? You some kind of angel or something?"

110. All he knew was that "Cryogenics" was written on the door in large red letters, and no matter how hard he tried, he couldn't get warm.

111. "I'm a lawyer, not your priest," he shouted.

112. The dragon opened his eye…

113. Light streaked across the sky, and the following sonic boom had him running towards…

114. The battering ram made short work of the door. Splintered wood littered the hallway…

115. Everyone seemed so happy at the celebration, but with every smiling face she encountered, she seemed to feel worse.

116. "I can cook," she volunteered.
    "Risking my life wasn't on the agenda for tonight," he…

117. He tried to open the locked door for a third time without using a key. She eyed him and rolled her eyes, stifling a…

118. The salt air stung his eyes as…

119. "That's not creepy at all," she quipped.

120. Resigned, he tossed the remnants into the trash can...

121. With the bartender unconscious, he helped himself to the...

122. The crime scene had been contaminated by...

123. When they tore down the wall, they discovered...

124. When the siren shattered the quiet of night, the...

125. "You are a genius!" he cried, jumping up and dashing to...

126. The bridge swayed in the fierce wind, causing...

127. Cloying was the only way the smell could be described.

128. "You wanna take a chance and check it out?" she asked, with raised brows.

129. Killing wasn't the problem, it was the...

130. It wasn't until water started filling the car that true panic set in.

131. *Wasn't that the guy on the news?*, he thought. But it was too late.

132. "In what world would that be okay?" she spat.

133. The mall was packed with frenzied shoppers making last minute purchases.

134. Their reunion was what others write epic stories about. They...

135. The kiss was a little too eager and the lips a little too firm to be believed as...

136. Pirates, complete with eye patches and missing teeth...

137. "I plan to use your back as my footstool when I break you," he growled.

138. The carriage looked as if it belonged to gypsies, the tapestries and...

139. When the door opened, the candles were snuffed, and she vacillated between...

140. The vibrant pops of color stunned the onlookers in a...

Prompt # _____ Your Title: _____

Prompt # _____ Your Title: _____

Prompt # _____ Your Title: _____

_____

_____

_____

_____

_____

_____

_____

_____

_____

_____

_____

_____

_____

_____

_____

_____

_____

_____

_____

_____

_____

_____

_____

_____

Prompt # _____ Your Title: _____

_____

_____

_____

_____

_____

_____

_____

_____

_____

_____

_____

_____

_____

_____

_____

_____

_____

_____

_____

_____

Prompt # _____ Your Title: _____

Prompt # _____ Your Title: _____

# Use These Phrases

## 141. Choose and use at least six of these ten phrases:

| | |
|---|---|
| the elevator hissed shut | trudging forward |
| whipped a tear away | stinging the senses |
| choked a laugh | chest heaving |
| sweeping gestures | boots thudded on the ground |
| should've been simple | never take for granted |

## 142. Choose and use at least seven of these ten phrases:

| | |
|---|---|
| hummed with | dizzying height |
| slick surface | like a slide under the microscope |
| moved woodenly | pushed to his/her feet |
| surged past | ugly sort of cry |
| puffed with pride | yowling discontent |

## 143. Choose and use at least eight of these ten phrases:

| | |
|---|---|
| burst of laughter | warm amber light |
| sway of the breeze | floral and citrus permeated |
| filled with grandeur | coaxed it out |
| inviting glow | nostalgic feeling |
| tisked with disapproval | skittered to the side |

## 144. Choose and use at least nine of these ten phrases:

| industrial floors | increased anxiety |
|---|---|
| lock flicked shut | silence was bloated |
| seemed impossible | snick of the door |
| ice spreading through | wrist awkwardly |
| drone of traffic | hope guttered |

**145. Choose and use at least nine of these ten phrases:**

| | |
|---|---|
| lava lamp | bustling crowd |
| swirling confusion | sour smell |
| wide expanse | thick shag carpet |
| knowing smile | pricked my memory |
| clunk of heavy shoes | jingle of keys |

# Choose a Path

**146.** **Her mischievous grin deepened as she opened her hand to reveal ...**

- ☐ eight brightly colored pills.
- ☐ a fist full of lottery tickets.
- ☐ a note from a secret admirer.
- ☐ car keys.
- ☐ a ring.

**147.** **He stared at his hands in disbelief as...**

- ☐ they had aged twenty years over night.
- ☐ there were fresh tattoos across his palms.
- ☐ they were covered in blood.
- ☐ small creatures no bigger than his pinky finger were latched on.
- ☐ his child had written "I love you" in magic marker.

**148.  The rampant rumors about the...**

- ☐  promotion
- ☐  breakup
- ☐  politician
- ☐  wide-spread famine
- ☐  genetic research

**149.  They handed over <u>the report</u> with grim faces...**

- ☐  stock report or quarter financials
- ☐  travel expense report
- ☐  grade report
- ☐  police report
- ☐  internet activity report

_____

_____

_____

_____

_____

_____

_____

_____

_____

_____

_____

_____

_____

_____

_____

_____

_____

_____

## 150. The tattered envelope contained...

- ☐ an old love letter.
- ☐ a report card.
- ☐ a lawsuit.
- ☐ a large or small check.
- ☐ a severed finger.

_____

_____

_____

_____

_____

_____

_____

_____

_____

_____

_____

_____

_____

_____

_____

_____

_____

## 151. He stared at the vial...

- ☐ of blue liquid, knowing it was the key to everything.
- ☐ and wondered if anyone knew he had it.
- ☐ praying it was the antidote.
- ☐ in a daze after running all of the samples in the lab.
- ☐ in the museum case, keeping an eye on security.

# Chart It

Fill out the chart and write the back story.

## Writing Challenge:

Use as few adverbs as possible. Consider "—ly" the enemy!

152. Create a wanted poster and write the crime that inspired it.

# Wanted

Name:

| Height: | Weight: | Build: |
|---|---|---|
| Eye Color: | Eye Shape: | Ear Shape: |
| Hair Color: | Hair Texture: | Hair Length: |
| Face Shape: | Lip Shape: | |

Other distinguishing features:

Last seen wearing:

153. **Pick a supporting character from one of your stories and write their origin.**

☐ Sidekick ☐ Love Interest ☐ Mentor ☐ Fool ☐ Nemesis

|  | Name | Meaning |
|---|---|---|
| First |  |  |
| Last |  |  |

## PHYSICAL DESCRIPTION

| Gender: | Age: | Height: |
|---|---|---|
| Eye Color: | Hair Color: | Weight & Body Shape: |
| Nationality: | Skin Tone: | Voice: |
| Facial Expression/Physical Ticks/Other: | | |

## INTERNAL DECRIPTION

| Personality Type: | |
|---|---|
| Strengths/Talents/Powers/Skills: | Flaws/Weaknesses/Limitations: |
| Backstory: (Why do we need this character?) | |

154. **Pick a supporting character from one of your stories and write their origin.**

□ Sidekick □ Love Interest □ Mentor □ Fool □ Nemesis

|  | Name | Meaning |
|---|---|---|
| First |  |  |
| Last |  |  |

## PHYSICAL DESCRIPTION

| Gender: | Age: | Height: |
|---|---|---|
| Eye Color: | Hair Color: | Weight & Body Shape: |
| Nationality: | Skin Tone: | Voice: |
| Facial Expression/Physical Ticks/Other: | | |

## INTERNAL DECRIPTION

| Personality Type: | |
|---|---|
| Strengths/Talents/Powers/Skills: | Flaws/Weaknesses/Limitations: |
| Backstory: (Why do we need this character?) | |

## 155. Pick a supporting character from one of your stories and write their origin.

☐ Sidekick ☐ Love Interest ☐ Mentor ☐ Fool ☐ Nemesis

|  | Name | Meaning |
|---|---|---|
| First |  |  |
| Last |  |  |

## PHYSICAL DESCRIPTION

| Gender: | Age: | Height: |
|---|---|---|
| Eye Color: | Hair Color: | Weight & Body Shape: |
| Nationality: | Skin Tone: | Voice: |
| Facial Expression/Physical Ticks/Other: | | |

## INTERNAL DECRIPTION

| Personality Type: | |
|---|---|
| Strengths/Talents/Powers/Skills: | Flaws/Weaknesses/Limitations: |
| Backstory: (Why do we need this character?) | |

## 156. Create a character with some kind of medical condition.

**MEDICAL HISTORY AND SCREENING FORM**

### General Information

Participant:

Name _____

Birth date _____

**Marital Status:** _____ **Sex:** _____

**Education:** _____

**Occupation:**

Position _____Employer

### Reason for today's visit? _____

_____

_____

### Present Medical History

**Check those questions to which you answer yes (leave the others blank).**

- ☐ Has a doctor ever said your blood pressure was too high?
- ☐ Do you ever have pain in your chest or heart?
- ☐ Does your heart often race?
- ☐ Are your ankles often badly swollen?
- ☐ Do you often have difficulty breathing?

**Comments:** _____

_____

_____

_____

**Do you now have or have you recently experienced:**

- ☐ Chronic, recurrent, or morning cough?
- ☐ Episode of coughing up blood?
- ☐ Increased anxiety or depression?
- ☐ Problems with recurrent fatigue, trouble sleeping, or increased irritability?
- ☐ Migraine or recurrent headaches?
- ☐ Pain in your legs after walking short distances?

- [ ] Foot problems?
- [ ] Back problems?
- [ ] Stomach or intestinal problems, such as recurrent heartburn, ulcers, constipation, or diarrhea?
- [ ] Significant vision or hearing problems?
- [ ] Recent change in a wart or a mole?
- [ ] Glaucoma or increased pressure in the eyes?
- [ ] Exposure to loud noises for long periods?
- [ ] Persistent pain or problems walking after you have fallen?
- [ ] Eye conditions such as bleeding in the retina or detached retina?

**Comments:** _____
_____
_____
_____

List hospitalizations, including dates of and reasons for hospitalization: _____
_____
_____

List any drug allergies:_____
_____
_____

**Past Medical History**

**Check those questions to which your answer is yes (leave others blank).**

- [ ] Heart attack, if so, how many years ago? _____
- [ ] Diabetes or abnormal blood-sugar tests
- [ ] Dizziness or fainting spells
- [ ] Epilepsy or seizures
- [ ] Scarlet Fever
- [ ] Infectious mononucleosis
- [ ] Bronchitis
- [ ] Asthma
- [ ] Abnormal chest X-ray
- [ ] Injuries to back, arms, legs or joint
- [ ] Broken bones
- [ ] Jaundice or gall bladder problems

**Comments:**_____
_____
_____
_____


## Family Medical History

**Father:** ☐ Alive     Current age _____   ☐ Excellent   ☐Good   ☐Fair   ☐Poor

Reason for poor health: _____

☐ Deceased     Age at death _____

Cause of death: _____

**Mother:** ☐ Alive     Current age _____   ☐ Excellent   ☐Good   ☐Fair   ☐Poor

Reason for poor health: _____

☐ Deceased     Age at death _____

Cause of death: _____

**Siblings:**

Number of brothers _____ Number of sisters _____ Age range _____

Health problems _____


Any other information that would be relevant to this visit?

_____
_____
_____
_____
_____
_____

# Dialogue Prompts

**A few tips before we start:**

- ☐ Avoid using the characters' names too much in dialogue.
- ☐ Make sure not all of your characters sound the same.
- ☐ Try not to have characters parrot or repeat the previous sentence.

## Writing Challenge:

Use as few adverbs as possible.

☐ Generally, people don't speak in complete sentences. Use some fragments.
☐ Play with dialect and the way your characters use contractions.
☐ Restarts, stumbles, and stutters can improve emotional scenes.

157. He forced his way into the room. "Did you do it?"

"W-What do you mean? I didn't d—"

"The bag! Did you take it?"

_____

_____

_____

_____

_____

_____

_____

_____

_____

_____

_____

_____

_____

_____

_____

_____

_____

_____

_____

_____

_____

158. "Mommy, it's under the bed."

"Don't look, sweetie."

"But—"

159. She gazed down her nose at me like I was nothing. "I see you have failed."

"No. I didn't."

Her grin was icy.

160. "You cleared out your desk?"

"I was going to tell you."

"Yet, you didn't."

161. "It is so good to see you." She beamed.

"You've gained weight."

_____

_____

_____

_____

_____

_____

_____

_____

_____

_____

_____

_____

_____

_____

_____

_____

_____

_____

_____

_____

162. "But I stayed up all night to finish it. This isn't fair."

"And I'm supposed to be moved by this?"

_____

_____

_____

_____

_____

_____

_____

_____

_____

_____

_____

_____

_____

_____

_____

_____

_____

_____

_____

_____

163. "You know what our parents would say?"

"Something cliché like, 'waste not, want not'?"

"No, 'just use the rocket launcher and be done with it.'"

_____

_____

_____

_____

_____

_____

_____

_____

_____

_____

_____

_____

_____

_____

_____

_____

_____

_____

_____

_____

_____

164. "I'll show them," he raged.

"Maybe you should sleep on it."

# Fill in the Blank: 49 Possibilities

**165. When the song came on, I could smell the** _____ **from that night and could feel** _____ .

| Blank One | Blank Two |
|---|---|
| pine | the hammering of my heart |
| wisteria | his/her hands on me |
| vomit | the bite of the handcuffs |
| stale liquor | the joy of celebration |
| fruity bubblegum | the lightheartedness of childhood |
| birthday cake | the burn of hard work |
| bleach | the sheen of sweat on my forehead |

166. There were only three minutes left before the _____,

filling me with _____.

| Blank One | Blank Two |
|---|---|
| bomb blew | murderous rage |
| timer went off | bubbling excitement |
| class bell rang | unfathomable relief |
| launch | the need to destroy |
| surprise | paralyzing fear |
| shark feeding | the desire to go straight to bed |
| shift change | uneasiness |

_____

_____

_____

_____

_____

_____

_____

_____

_____

_____

_____

_____

_____

_____

_____

_____

_____

**167. The water was** _____ **as**

_____ .

| Blank One | Blank Two |
|---|---|
| bubbling and warm | the animals gathered to drink |
| swirling in the cauldron | we eased into the hot tub |
| at low tide | I crawled across the desert |
| flowing steadily | the sun melted into the ocean |
| sparkling in my glass | we realized not all would survive |
| my only lifeline | we walked along the ragged shore |
| held back | the witches cast their spell |

168. It spread _____, and everyone around

   _____.

| Blank One | Blank Two |
| --- | --- |
| like a virus | moved towards the sweet aroma |
| its wings | avoided the sprouting vines |
| through the water | bounced with renewed energy |
| through the air | gagged and fell dead |
| joy | cautiously prepared to run |
| like it was sentient | bowed to the angel in fear |
| with wicked glee | understood what it meant |

# Traditional Prompts

## Self-Discovery

**Many of these are well-worn, but creativity can spring from old favorites. These may help you unlock something inside yourself, make students think deeply about themselves, serve as interview questions, or help develop a character background.**

169. Pick a moment in your childhood when you were truly scared and write about it.

170. If you could change one thing about yourself, what would it be? Why?

171. If you had a superpower, what would it be and why?

172. What is your most positive trait? Why is that important?

173. What can't you do without?

174. If your house was burning down, what would you save and why?

175. If you were an animal, which one would you choose and why?

176. Would you prefer to be stranded in the mountains or on the coast? Explain.

177. What does no one know about you?

178. What are you judgmental about (or not judgmental)?

179. Who is your ideal mate? What qualities would he/she have?

180. Write a letter to your future self.

181. Write a list of ten reasons you should be happy or thankful.

182. If you could acquire any talent with little to no training, what would it be?

183. What is your favorite time of day and why?

184. What advice would you give to someone younger than you?

185. What do you wish your parents understood about you?

186. If you could be any celebrity for a day, who would you be? And why.

187. Thoughts while brushing your teeth...

188. Write a bucket list with twenty things you intend to complete before you die.

189. If you had the chance to travel in space, would you? Why or why not?

190. Write an itinerary for the perfect day.

191. If you could solve one worldwide crisis, what would it be and why?

192. You are going to a cosplay convention. How do you dress?

193. If it's not about you, what is it about?

194. When I smell _____, it makes me think of _____ and...

195. What is your favorite motivational quote or saying? How has it inspired you?

196. When you wake up, you discover that you are inside a children's cartoon or television show. What's the show and what do you do?

197. While drifting off to sleep, you stare at a hole in your socks. How does that impact your dreams that night?

198. If you could design your bedroom in any style or color without worrying about money, what would it look like? Explain the details like it really exists.

199. Do you prefer being hot or cold? Write a story when you were too hot or too cold. Include smells and sounds, as well as the feelings.

200. Failure often teaches more than success. When have you failed, and what did you learn from it? For added challenge, try telling it as a parable.

201. You have $100,000 to spend in one day. At the end of the day, you can't have anything left-over except photos. What would you do?

202. Think of a trip you took when you were younger. Why did it make such an impression?

203. In what conditions are you most creative? At home? A coffee shop? What time of day? Music?

204. Describe your home, but do it as if you were a character in either a horror film or action comedy.

205. Write a short bio about yourself, but through the eyes of several different types of writers: children's, crime, dystopian, fantasy, historical, humor, military, mystery, non-fiction, romance, screen, steampunk, thriller, or young adult.

# If You Were

If you were ___, who/what would you be? Explain by telling a story using vivid verbs and sensory images.

206. A piece of clothing

207. A piece of art

208. A famous landmark

209. A land-dwelling animal

210. A fish

211. A bird

212. An extinct mammal

213. An entrée

214. A dessert

215. A piece of flatware

216. A super-hero

217. A super-villain

218. A public servant

219. A world leader

220. A teacher

221. A mountain

222. A river

223. An ocean or sea

224. A car

225. A natural disaster (earthquake, tornado, hurricane, tsunami, etc.)

# Mixed Bag

**A little mix of everything to keep it interesting.**

226. Pick three objects in the room that are the same color and write a story about how they are related.

227. You wake up and your skin is bright green. There is no indication that it is going to change anytime soon, and there is no way that you can stay home and hide.

228. What happens after a major natural disaster? Tell it from the perspective of an unreliable narrator.

229. Pick any fairytale or folktale and rewrite the ending.

230. You help your family move and find adoption papers—they aren't your parents.

231. You are a fake superhero with no real powers. How would you fool the world?

232. Two strangers switch bags by accident; the fallout is catastrophic.

233. You attend your first meeting of Assassins Anonymous.

234. Solar flares cause the weather to change dramatically all over the earth.

235. You are offered the job of being Death for a day.

236. When you are dusting, you knock a plant off of the shelf and find a tiny camera.

237. After working out, you hit the showers. When you return, all of your clothes are gone, including your sweaty habiliments.

238. While at the traveling circus, a clown cocks his head to the side and gives you a sinister grin.

239. When at the ATM, you find that there is an extra $50,000 in your account.

240. After being stranded, hitchhiking is the only option.

241. The once beautiful garden was a gnarled tapestry of the wrongdoing.

242. The ribbon in her hair looked like snakeskin—and then it moved.

# Make a List Of...

243. Reasons to sleep in

244. Other words for whisper

245. Colors, but give them creative names (i.e. Black = Midnight Velvet)

246. Reasons why it is okay to lie

247. Reasons why it is important to tell the truth

248. Character names that you like and a one sentence description

249. Places where interesting people to live

250. A dozen clichés to avoid

251. A dozen of the best lines you have ever heard

252. Reasons a librarian would suddenly have to leave town

253. Ten goals you have for the month

254. Descriptions of how different foods smell

255. Fifteen uses for a paperclip

256. Reasons to refuse to date someone

257. Twenty rules that shouldn't exist

258. Twenty rules that should exist

259. Ten reason forgiveness is more powerful than resentment

260. Things the universe is conspiring against you

261. Plot devices you will avoid

262. Character archetypes you want to explore

263. Things you can do when the power goes out

264. Books you plan on reading to make you a better writer

Prompt # _____ Your Title: _____

Prompt # _____ Your Title: _____

Prompt # _____ Your Title: _____

Prompt # _____ Your Title: _____

Prompt # _____ Your Title: _____

Prompt # _____ Your Title: _____

Prompt # _____ Your Title: _____

# Haiku

## A Practice in Brevity

## Writing Challenge:

Diversify your topics and include haikus: about a friend, a family member, and something romantic. Then tap into some emotions: happiness, sadness, indifference, and need.

Haikus are a great way to practice precise language. They are three lines long. The first line is five syllables, the second is seven, and the third five. Here are a few samples.

I wrote this one for a friend on her birthday:

I liken Danielle, <sup>5</sup>
To a lively summers day. <sup>7</sup>
Filled with bright laughter. <sup>5</sup>
--Robin Woods

They can be romantic:

In one fleeting glance, <sup>5</sup>
I saw your heart and you mine <sup>7</sup>
Entangled in fate. <sup>5</sup>
--Robin Woods

Or even sinister:

You are a dark thing— <sup>5</sup>
Twisted, bent, and craving more. <sup>7</sup>
Waiting to devour. <sup>5</sup>
--Robin Woods

265. About nature:

_____ 5

_____ 7

_____ 5

266. About love:

_____

_____

_____

267. About loss:

_____

_____

_____

268. About joy:

_____

_____

_____

269. About friendship:

_____

_____

_____

270. About the city:

_____

_____

_____

# Journal

# Reference

# Character Traits

All characters, even good ones, should have some reasonable flaws. And in turn, characters that are purely evil often appear fake. It is best to have a healthy mix of believable traits. Here is a list to get you thinking:

**Positive Traits**

| | | | | |
|---|---|---|---|---|
| Adaptable | Accepting | Adventurous | Affectionate | Amiable |
| Alert | Astute | Benevolent | Brave | Charismatic |
| Creative | Decisive | Dependable | Diplomatic | Disciplined |
| Earnest | Efficient | Empathetic | Enthusiastic | Ethical |
| Fair | Forgiving | Good-hearted | Gracious | Happy |
| Hard-working | Independent | Insightful | Intelligent | Just |
| Leader | Loving | Nurturing | Orderly | Patient |
| Passionate | Persuasive | Playful | Responsible | Resourceful |
| Self-aware | Spunky | Strong | Studious | Supportive |
| Tactful | Tenacious | Unselfish | Watchful | Wise |

**Negative Traits**

| | | | | |
|---|---|---|---|---|
| Abusive | Addictive | Aggressive | Antisocial | Apathetic |
| Argumentative | Belligerent | Callous | Cantankerous | Childish |
| Clingy | Closed-minded | Cocky | Compulsive | Cowardly |
| Cruel | Cynical | Dangerous | Deceitful | Defensive |
| Degrading | Destructive | Disloyal | Egocentric | Evil |
| Fearful | Fixated | Flaky | Foolish | Forgetful |
| Hostile | Hung-up | Insecure | Loner | Megalomaniacal |
| Neurotic | Phobic | Perfectionist | Pessimistic | Prejudiced |
| Manipulative | Selfish | Self-destructive | Stubborn | Sulker |
| Touchy | Unreceptive | Vengeful | Whiney | Withdrawn |

# Character Appearance Charts

| | | | | | |
|---|---|---|---|---|---|
| **Eye Color** | Blue | Sky Blue | Baby Blue | Electric Blue | Cornflower |
| | Brown | Chestnut | Chocolate | Cognac | Amber |
| | Green | Sea Green | Moss Green | Jade | Emerald |
| | Grey | Silver | Gunmetal Grey | Charcoal | Black |
| | Hazel | Russet | Nut | Honey | Yellow |
| | Lavender | Other: | | | |
| **Eye Shape** | Almond | Round | Drooping | Hooded | Close-set |
| | Wide-set | Deep-set | Protruding | Sleepy | Squinting |
| | Down-turned | Other: | | | |
| **Skin Tone** | Fair | Ivory | Porcelain | Milk | Snow |
| | Ruddy | Rose | Peach | Ochre | Golden |
| | Olive | Khaki | Toffee | Honey | Tawny |
| | Dark | Ebony | Sepia | Russet | Mahogany |
| | Other: | | | | |
| **Body Shape** | Triangle | Rectangle | Hourglass | Rounded | Diamond |
| | Inverted Triangle | Barrel | Willowy | Husky | Wiry |
| | Other: | | | | |
| **Facial Shapes** | Oval | Rectangle | Square | Heart | Oblong |
| | Egg | Diamond | Triangle | Narrow | Block-like |
| | Other: | | | | |
| **Hair Color** | Black | Dark Brown | Medium Brown | Ash Brown | Golden Brown |
| | Red | Auburn | Copper | Strawberry | Cinnamon |
| | Blond | Platinum | White | Silver | Grey |
| | Other: | | | | |
| Notes: | | | | | |

# Avoid Language that Offends

Sometimes we don't think about the language we have grown up hearing. Try to avoid language that is belittling. Of course, if you have a sexist or racist character, use it in their dialogue.

## Samples of Sexist, Discriminatory, and Stereotypical Language

| Original | Alternate |
| --- | --- |
| Authoress | Author |
| Chairman, Chairwoman | Chairperson, Person, Coordinator |
| Common man | Ordinary people, average person |
| Congressman | Congressional Representative, Legislator |
| Fireman | Firefighter |
| Housewife | Homemaker |
| Invalid | Disabled |
| Mailman | Mail Carrier, Postal Worker |
| Male Nurse | Nurse |
| Mankind | Humanity, Human Race, Human Beings, People |
| Man-made | Manufactured, Synthetic |
| Policewoman, Policeman | Police officer |
| Six Man-hours | Six Working-hours, Six Staff-hours |
| Stewardess, Steward | Flight Attendant |
| To Man | To Staff, To Operate |
| Weatherman | Meteorologist, Forecaster |
| Workman | Worker, Laborer |
| Notes: | |

# Strong Words to Know and Use

| | | |
|---|---|---|
| adversary | grueling | recuperate |
| aplomb | gusto habitation | replenish |
| apprehensive | hasten | repugnant |
| aptitude | headway | restitution |
| attentive | ignite | scurry |
| banish | illuminate | sabotage |
| barricade | impending | scarcity |
| bluff | imperious | serenity |
| brackish | jabber | sociable |
| brandish | jargon | somber |
| circumference | jostle | specimen |
| commotion | jut | stamina |
| concoction | kindle | subside |
| conspicuous | knoll | swagger |
| contortion | luminous | swarm |
| counter | malleable | tactic |
| cunning | materialize | terse |
| debris | meander | translucent |
| defiance | meticulous | uncanny |
| deft | misgiving | unsightly |
| destination | momentum | versatile |
| diminish | monotonous | vigilant |
| disdain | multitude | vulnerable |
| dismal | muster | waft |
| dispel | narrate | waver |
| eavesdrop | obscure | weather |
| egregious | ominous | zeal |
| ember | outlandish | |
| emerge | persistent | My list: |
| engross | pertinent | |
| exasperation | plenteous | |
| exhilarate | potential | |
| falter | precipice | |
| foresight | pristine | |
| fragrance | quell | |
| furtive | recluse | |

# Tastes and Aromas

When you are writing, try to incorporate all four of the senses in your work. Here is a cheat sheet for tastes and smells:

| Positive | Neutral | Negative | Spices | Florals (Most Fragrant) |
|---|---|---|---|---|
| Aromatic | Acidic | Biting | Cajun | Angel's Trumpet |
| Citrusy | Acrid | Bitter | Cinnamon | Flowering Plum |
| Comforting | Airy | Decay | Clove | Heliotrope |
| Crisp | Ancient | Dirty | Coriander | Honeysuckle |
| Delicate | Brackish | Fetid | Cumin | Jasmin |
| Delicious | Burnt | Foul | Dill | Lavender |
| Exquisite | Delicate | Funky | Pepper | Lilac |
| Fragrant | Feminine | Gamy | Sage | Mexican Orange |
| Fresh | Fermented | Harsh | Thyme | Mock Orange |
| Fruity | Masculine | Moldy | Basil | Rose |
| Full-bodied | Floral | Musty | Barbeque | Star Magnolia |
| Hard | Humid | Nasty | Bay Leaf | Sweet Peas |
| Heady | Light | Noxious | Curry | Tuberose |
| Juicy | Medicinal | Old | Anise | **Household Smells** |
| Lemony | Medium | Pungent | Caraway Seed | |
| Rich | Mellow | Putrid | Cardamom | Babies |
| Savory | Metallic | Rancid | Cayenne | "Boy" Smell |
| Sharp | Mild | Rank | Cumin | Bacon |
| Succulent | Minty | Repulsive | Dill | BBQ |
| Sugary | Moist | Rotting | Fennel | Beer |
| Sweet | Musky | Skunky | Garlic | Books |
| Tangy | Nippy | Sour | Ginger | Bread |
| Tart | Nutty | Spoiled | Mace | Burning Wood |
| Tempting | Peppery | Stagnant | Marjoram | Chocolate |
| Warm | Perfumed | Stale | Mint | Cinnamon |
| Woody | Salty | Stench | Mustard | Citrus |
| Zesty | Woodsy | Stinking | Onion | Coconut |
| Zingy | Yeasty | Stuffy | Orange Peel | Coffee |
| | | | Lemon Peel | Cut Grass |
| Other: | Other: | Other: | Nutmeg | Dirty Laundry |
| | | | Rosemary | Fresh–baked Cookies |
| | | | Saffron | Fresh Laundry |
| | | | Turmeric | Pine |
| | | | Vanilla | Soap |

# Words for Sounds

Add appeal to your writing by making a splash with descriptive sound words.

| | | | | | |
|---|---|---|---|---|---|
| Ahem | Clatter | Grind | Pound | Splash | Tweet |
| Baa | Click | Groan | Pow | Splat | Vip |
| Babble | Clink | Gulp | Pulsing | Splinter | Vroom |
| Bang | Clomp | Gurgle | Purr | Sputter | Wail |
| Bark | Clonk | Guzzle | Quack | Squawk | Wallop |
| Beat | Clop | Hammer | Racket | Squeak | Warble |
| Beep | Cluck | Hiss | Rap | Squish | Whack |
| Bellow | Clunk | Hoot | Ratchet | Stomp | Wham |
| Blare | Crackle | Howl | Rattle | Suck | Wheeze |
| Blast | Crash | Hubbub | Revved | Swish | Whicker |
| Blip | Creak | Hum | Ring | Swoop | Whinny |
| Blop | Crinkle | Jangle | Rip | Swoosh | Whip |
| Blow | Crunch | Jingle | Roar | Tap | Whir |
| Boing | Din | Kerplunk | Rumble | Tatter | Whisper |
| Bong | Ding | Knock | Rushing | Tee-hee | Whistle |
| Boo | Discord | Lash | Rustle | Throb | Whiz |
| Boom | Drip | Mew | Scream | Thud | Whoosh |
| Bop | Drone | Mewl | Screech | Thump | Woof |
| Bray | Drum | Murmur | Scuff | Thunder | Woot |
| Bubble | Eek | Neigh | Shriek | Thwack | Yabber |
| Burp | Fanfare | Oink | Shuffle | Tick | Yahoo |
| Buzz | Fizz | Ooze | Sizzle | Tinkle | Yammer |
| Cacophony | Fizzle | Patter | Slam | Titter | Yap |
| Cha-Ching | Flick | Peal | Slap | Tock | Yawp |
| Cheep | Fling | Peep | Slop | Tolling | Yelp |
| Chime | Flop | Pew | Slurp | Toot | Yip |
| Chirp | Fracas | Pitter-patter | Smack | Trill | Yowl |
| Chug | Giggle | Plink | Snap | Tromp | Zap |
| Clack | Glug | Plod | Snicker | Trumpet | Zing |
| Clamor | Glurp | Plop | Snigger | Tsk | Zip |
| Clang | Gnashing | Plunk | Snip | Tumult | Zonk |
| Clank | Gobble | Poof | Snort | Tut | Zoom |
| Clap | Grating | Pop | Spatter | Twang | Zzzz |

# Synonyms

As you are editing, it is important to pay attention to repetition. Much of the tinkering with words will come with editing, but I love using synonym sheets to cut down on the editing later, as well as to inspire me.

---

## Emotions

### Other words for **Happy**

Alluring, amused, appealing, appeased, blissful, blithe, carefree, charmed, cheeky, chipper, chirpy, content, convivial, delighted, elated, electrified, ecstatic, enchanted, enthusiastic, exultant, excited, fantastic, fulfilled, glad, gleeful, glowing, gratified, idyllic, intoxicating, jolly, joyful, joyous, jovial, jubilant, light, lively, merry, mirthful, overjoyed, pleased, pleasant, radiant, sparkling, savoured, satisfied, serene, sunny, thrilled, tickled, up, upbeat, winsome, wonderful.

### Other words for **SAD**

Aching, agitated, anguished, anxious, bleak, bothered, brooding, bugged, chagrined, cheerless, darkly, disillusioned, disappointed, disenchanted, disheartened, dismayed, distraught, dissatisfied, despondent, doleful, failed, faint, frustrated, glazed, gloomy, glowering, haunted, hopeless, languid, miserable, pained, perturbed, sour, suffering, sullen, thwarted, tormented, troubled, uneasy, unsettled, upset, vacant, vexed, wan, woeful, wounded.

### Other words for **Mad**

Affronted, aggravated, agitated, angered, annoyed, bitter, boiling, bothered, brooding, bugged, bummed, cantankerous, chafed, chagrined, crabby, cross, disgruntled, distraught, disturbed, enflamed, enraged, exasperated, fiery, fuming, furious, frantic, galled, goaded, hacked, heated, hostile, hot, huffy, ill-tempered, incensed, indignant, inflamed, infuriated, irate, ireful, irritated, livid, maddened, malcontent, miffed, nettled, offended, peeved, piqued, provoked, raging, resentful, riled, scowling, sore, sour, stung, taut, tense, tight, troubled, upset, vexed, wrathful.

### Other words for **Crying**

Bawling, blubbering, gushing, howling, lamenting, moaning, scream-crying, silent tears, sniffling, snivelling, sobbing, sorrowing, teary, wailing, weepy, woeful.

# Commonly Used Words

## Other words for ASKED

Appealed, begged, beckoned, beseeched, besieged, bid, craved, commanded, claimed, coaxed, challenged, charged, charmed, cross-examined, demanded, drilled, entreated, enchanted, grilled, implored, imposed, interrogated, invited, invoked, inquired, insisted, needled, ordered, pleaded, petitioned, picked, probed, pried, pressed, pumped, pursued, put through the wringer, put the screws down, questioned, queried, quizzed, requested, required, requisitioned, roasted, solicited, summoned, surveyed, sweated, urged, wanted, wheedled, wooed, worried, wondered.

## Other words for LAUGH

Break up, burst, cackle, chortle, chuckle, crack-up, crow, giggle, grin, guffaw, hee-haw, howl, peal, quack, roar, scream, shriek, snicker, snigger, snort, split one's sides, tee-hee, titter, whoop.

## Other Words for LOOK

Address, admire, attention, audit, babysit, beam, beholding, blink, bore, browse, burn, cast, check, comb, consider, contemplate, delve, detect, discover, disregard, distinguish, ensure, evil eye, examine, explore, eye, eyeball, ferret, fix, flash, forage, gander, gaze, get an eyeful, give the eye, glance, glare, glaze, glimmer, glimpse, glitter, gloat, goggle, grope, gun, have a gander, inquire, inspect, investigate, judge, keeping watch, leaf-through, leer, lock daggers on, look fixedly, look-see, marking, moon, mope, neglect, note, notice, noting, observe, ogle, once-over, peek, peep, peer, peg, peruse, poke into, scan, pout, probe, pry, quest, rake, recognize, reconnaissance, regard, regarding, renew, resemble, review, riffle, rubberneck, rummage, scan, scowl, scrutinize, search, seeing, sense, settle, shine, sift, simper, size-up, skim, slant, smile, smirk, snatch, sneer, speculative, spot, spy, squint, stare, study, sulk, supervise, surveillance, survey, sweep, take stock of, take in, trace, verify, view, viewing, watch, witness, yawp, zero in.

## Other words for REPLIED

Acknowledged, answered, argued, accounted, barked, bit, be in touch, boomeranged, comeback, countered, conferred, claimed, denied, echoed, feedback, fielded the question, get back to, growled, matched, parried, reacted, reciprocated, rejoined, responded, retorted, remarked, returned, retaliated, shot back, snapped, squelched, squared, swung, vacillated.

## Other words for **Sat**

Be seated, bear on, cover, ensconce, give feet a rest, grab a chair, have a place, have a seat, hunker, install, lie, park, perch, plop down, pose, posture, put it there, relax, remain, rest, seat, seat oneself, settle, squat, take a load off, take a place, take a seat.

## Other words for **Was/Were**   VERB (TO BE)

Abided, acted, be alive, befell, breathed, continued, coexisted, do, endured, ensued, existed, had been, happened, inhabited, lasted, lived, moved, obtained, occurred, persisted, prevailed, remained, rested, stood, stayed, survived, subsided, subsisted, transpired.

## Other words for **Walk**

Advance, amble, barge, bolt, bounce, bound, canter, charge, crawl, creep, dance, dash, escort, gallop, hike, hobble, hop, jog, jump, leap, limp, lope, lumber, meander, mosey, move, pad, pace march, parade, patrol, plod, prance, proceed, promenade, prowl, race, roam, rove, run, sashay, saunter, scamper, scramble, zip shuffle, skip, slink, slither, slog, sprint, stagger, step, stomp, stride, stroll, strut, stumble, swagger, thread, tiptoe, traipse, tramp, tread, trek, trip, trot, trudge, wade, wander.

## Other words for **Whisper**

Breathed, buzz, disclosed, exhaled, expressed, fluttered, gasped, hint, hiss, hum, hushed tone, intoned, lament, low voice, moaned, mouthed, mumble, murmur, mutter, puff, purred, reflected, ruffle, rumble, rush, said low, said softly, sigh, sob, undertone, utter, voiced, wheezed.

## Other words for **Went**

Abscond, ambled, approached, avoided, be off, beat it, bolted, bounced, bounded, bugged out, burst, carved, cleared out, crawled, crept, cruised, cut and run, danced, darted, dashed, decamped, deserted, disappeared, ducked out, escaped, evaded, exited, fared, fled, floated, flew, flew the coop, galloped, got away, got going, got lost, glided, go down, go south, hightailed, hit the road, hoofed it, hopped, hotfooted, hurdled, hustled, journeyed, jumped, leapt, left, lighted out, loped, lunged, made haste, made a break for it, made for, made off, made tracks, marched, moseyed, moved, muscled, neared, negotiated, paced, paraded, passed, pedalled, proceeded, progressed, pulled out, pulled, pushed off, pushed on, quitted, retired, retreated, rode, ran along, ran away, rushed, sashayed, scampered, scooted, scrammed, scurried, scuttled, set off, set out, shot, shouldered, shoved off, shuffled, skedaddled, skipped out, skipped, skirted, slinked, slipped, soared, split, sprang, sprinted, stole away, steered clear, stepped on it, strolled, strutted, scurried, swept, took a hike, took a powder, took flight, took leave, took off, threaded, toddled, tottered, trampled, travelled, traversed, trekked, trode, trudged, tumbled, vamoosed, vanished, vaulted, veered, walked off, wandered, weaved, wended, whisked, withdrew, wormed, zipped, zoomed.

# Other words for SAID

accused, acknowledged, added, announced, addressed, admitted, advised, affirmed, agreed, asked, avowed, asserted, answered, apologized, argued, assured, approved, articulated, alleged, attested, barked, bet, bellowed, babbled, begged, bragged, began, bawled, bleated, blurted, boomed, broke in, bugged, boasted, bubbled, beamed, burst out, believed, brought out, confided, crowed, coughed, cried, congratulated, complained, conceded, chorused, concluded, confessed, chatted, convinced, chattered, cheered, chided, chimed in, clucked, coaxed, commanded, cautioned, continued, commented, called, croaked, chuckled, claimed, choked, chortled, corrected, communicated, claimed, contended, criticized, construe,

dared, decided, disagreed, described, disclosed, drawled, denied, declared, demanded, divulged, doubted, denied, disputed, dictated, echoed, ended, exclaimed, explained, expressed, enunciated, expounded, emphasized, formulated, fretted, finished, gulped, gurgled, gasped, grumbled, groaned, guessed, gibed, giggled, greeted, growled, grunted, hinted, hissed, hollered, hypothesized, inquired, imitated, implied, insisted, interjected, interrupted, intoned, informed, interpreted, illustrated, insinuated, jeered, jested, joked, justified, lied, laughed, lisped, maintained, muttered, marveled, moaned, mimicked, mumble, modulated, murmured, mused, mentioned, mouthed, nagged, noted, nodded, noticed,

objected, observed, offered, ordered, owned up, piped, pointed out, panted, pondered, praised, prayed, puzzled, proclaimed, promised, proposed, protested, purred, pled, pleaded, put in, prevailed, parried, pressed, put forward, pronounced, pointed out, prescribed, popped off, persisted, protested, questioned, quavered, quipped, quoted, queried, rejected, reasoned, ranted, reassured, reminded, responded, recalled, returned, requested, roared, related, remarked, replied, reported, revealed, rebutted, retorted, repeated, reckoned, remembered, regarded, recited, resolved, reflected, ripped, rectified, reaffirmed,

snickered, sniffed, smirked, snapped, snarled, shot, sneered, sneezed, started, stated, stormed, sobbed, stuttered, suggested, surmised, sassed, sputtered, sniffled, snorted, spoke, stammered, squeaked, sassed, scoffed, scolded, screamed, shouted, sighed, smiled, sang, shrieked, shrilled, speculated, supposed, settled, solved, shot back, swore, stressed, spilled, told, tested, trilled, taunted, teased, tempted, theorized, threatened, tore, uttered, unveiled, urged, upheld, vocalized, voiced, vindicated, volunteered, vowed, vented, verbalized, warned, wailed, went on, wept, whimpered, whined, wondered, whispered, worried, warranted, yawned, yakked.

# My Synonym Lists:

# Other Notes & Research

# Books by Robin Woods

### Young Adult Fiction

*Allure: A Watcher Series Prequel*

*The Unintended: The Watcher Series Book One*

*The Nexus: The Watcher Series Book Two*

*The Sacrifice: The Watcher Series Book Three*

*The Fallen: Part One: Watcher Series Book Four*

*The Fallen: Part Two: Watcher Series Book Five*

### Non-Fiction

*Prompt Me Workbook & Journal*

*Prompt Me Again Workbook & Journal*

*Prompt Me More Workbook & Journal*

*Prompt Me Sci-Fi & Fantasy Workbook & Journal*

*Prompt Me Romance Workbook & Journal*

*Prompt Me Novel Fiction Writing Workbook & Journal*

*Prompt Me Horror & Thriller Workbook & Journal*

*Prompt Me Reading: Literary Analysis & Journal*

More Prompt Me Series in 2020: **Prompt Me Mystery & Suspense, Prompt Me Kids,** and more.

# About the Author

Robin Woods is a former high school and university instructor with two and a half decades of experience teaching English, literature, and writing. She earned a BA in English and an MA in education.

In addition to teaching, she has published six highly rated novels and has multiple projects in the works, including writing for a Hollywood producer.

When Ms. Woods isn't chasing her two elementary school kids around, she's spending time with her ever-patient husband

For more information and free resources, go to her website at:

www.RobinWoodsFiction.com

Made in the USA
Middletown, DE
11 January 2020